# A
# Treasury
## of
# *Wisdom*

Selected by
Helen Jaeger

LOYOLAPRESS.
CHICAGO

# Picture Acknowledgments

p. 7 © 1991, Photo SCALA, Florence (hereafter referred to as PSF). Padua, Museo Civico. *Young Lace Maker with Her Teacher*, Gabrielli, c. 1611–1706. p. 8 © 1990, PSF. Milan, Biblioteca Trivuiziana. Codex 2167 c. 13 v. the School. p. 11 © PSF. New York, Pierpont Morgan Library. *The Lord Answering Job out of the Whirlwind*, Blake, 1757–1827. p. 13 © 1990, PSF – courtesy of the Ministero Beni e Att. Culturali. Florence, Galleria Palatina. *The Broken Bridge*, Rosa, 1615–1673. pp. 14–15 © 1990, PSF – courtesy of the Ministero Beni e Att. Culturali. Florence, Galleria d'Arte Moderna. *Woodcutters*, Banti, 1824–1904. p. 16 © 1990, PSF. Ljubljana, Gallery of Modern Art. *The Sower*, Grohar, 1867–1911. p. 19 © 2003, PSF/HIP. London, British Library. *An Outdoor Feast*, c. 1605–c. 1615. p. 23 © 1990, PSF – courtesy of Comune di Pesaro/Servizio Musei. Pesaro, Musei Civici. *Eternal Father*, 1505 inv. 3999, Bellini, 1430–1516. p. 27 © 1990, PSF. St Petersburg, Hermitage Museum. *Young Woman and Little Girl at the Window (The Prayer)*, Laurent, 1763–1832. p. 29 © 1990, PSF. El Escorial, Monastery of San Lorenzo. *Jacob Among the Sheep*, Ribera, 1591–1652. p. 33 © 1990, PSF. Bergamo, Accademia Carrara. *Memory of Pain*, Pellizza da Volpedo, 1868–1907. p. 35 © 1990, PSF. Ljubljana, Gallery of Modern Art. *Apple Tree in Blossom*, Grohar, 1867–1911. p. 39 © 1998, PSF. Geneva, Musée d'Art Moderne. *Waiting for the Fishermen in Brittany*, Moret, 1856–1913. p. 42 © 1990, PSF. St Petersburg, Hermitage Museum. *Liberation of Saint Peter*, Murillo, 1618–1682. p. 44 © 1990, PSF – courtesy of the Ministero Beni e Att. Culturali. Florence, Galleria Palatina. *Girl with Lamp*, Schalcken, 1643–1706. p. 47 © 1990, PSF. St Petersburg, Hermitage Museum. *Return of the Prodigal Son*, Rembrandt, 1606–1669. p. 49 © 1992, PSF – courtesy of the Ministero Beni e Att. Culturali. Turin, Galleria Sabauda. *The Castle of Collegno with Effect of Storm*, Loo, 1743–1821. p. 53 © 1990, PSF. Feodosiya, Aivazovsky Gallery. *Shipwreck*, Aivazovsky, 1817–1900. p. 55 © 1992, PSF. Moscow, Tretyakov State Gallery. *Teremnoy Palace, the Door on the Golden Terrace*, Polienov, 1844–1927. p. 57 © 1990, PSF – courtesy of the Ministero Beni e Att. Culturali. Naples, Museo di Capodimonte. *The Shepherd Lass*, Michetti, 1851–1929. p. 59 © 1997, PSF. Venice, Doge's Palace. *Visions of the Hereafter: the Garden of Eden and the Ascent to Heaven*, Bosch c. 1450–1516. p. 60 © 1990, PSF. Antwerp, Koninklijk Museum voor Schone Kunsten. *Summer*, Grimmer, c. 1573–1619. p. 65 © 1990, PSF. Paris, Musée d'Orsay. *The Angelus*, Millet, 1814–1875. p. 67 © 1990, PSF. Siena, Monte dei Paschi Coll. *Christ Carrying the Cross*, Sodoma, 1477–1549. p. 68 © 1998, PSF. Moscow, Pushkin Museum. *The Gust of Wind*, Corot, 1796–1875. p. 71 © 1990, PSF. Vatican, Sistine Chapel (Walls). *Sermon on the Mount and Healing of the Leper*, Rosselli, 1439–1507. p. 74 © 1993, PSF – courtesy of the Ministero Beni e Att. Culturali. Parma, Galleria Nazionale. *The Healing of the Blind Man*, El Greco, 1541–1614. p. 77 © 1990, PSF. Paris, Petit Palais. *Demoiselles de la Seine*, Courbet, 1819–1877. p. 79 © 1990, PSF. Paris, Louvre. *The Money Changer and His Wife*, 1514, Massys, c. 1466–1530. p. 81 © 1990, PSF. Venice, Galleria d'Arte Moderna. *Death of a Chick*, Nono, 1850–1918. p. 85 © 1990, PSF – courtesy of the Ministero Beni e Att. Culturali. Florence, Galleria d'Arte Moderna. *Country Life*, Focardi, 1864–1934. p. 86 © 2001, PSF – courtesy of the Ministero Beni e Att. Culturali. Florence, Galleria Palatina. *The Lost Drachma*, Feti, 1589–1624. p. 88 © 1990, PSF – courtesy of the Ministero Beni e Att. Culturali. Florence, Galleria d'Arte Moderna. *In the Fields*, Ferroni, 1835–1912. p. 93 © 1990, PSF. Pushkin Museum, Moscow. *The Archangel Raphael with Bishop Domonte*, Murillo, 1618–1682. p. 94 © 1990, PSF. Munich, Alte Pinakothek. *Ascension*, Rembrandt, 1606–1669.

*To Ben*

# LOYOLAPRESS.

3441 N. ASHLAND AVENUE
CHICAGO, ILLINOIS 60657
(800) 621-1008
WWW.LOYOLABOOKS.ORG

First published in North America in 2005 by Loyola Press.
ISBN 0-8294-2160-2

### Acknowledgments

11, 20, 32, 40, 44, 50, 60, 64, 82, 92: Scripture quotations
taken from the Authorized Version of the Bible (The King James
Bible), the rights in which are vested in the Crown, reproduced
by permission of the Crown's Patentee, Cambridge University
Press. 15, 24, 36, 41, 56, 64, 76, 78, 80, 82, 95: Scripture
quotations taken from the Good News Bible published by The
Bible Societies/HarperCollins Publishers, copyright © 1966,
1971, 1976, 1992 American Bible Society. 17, 25, 52, 63, 72,
79: Scripture quotations taken from the Revised Standard
Version published by HarperCollins Publishers, copyright ©
1989 by the Division of Christian Education of the National
Council of the Churches of Christ in the USA, and used by
permission. All rights reserved. 40, 54, 83, 87, 91: Scripture
quotations taken from The New Revised Standard Version of
the Bible, Anglicized Edition, copyright © 1989, 1995 by the
Division of Christian Education of the National Council of
the Churches of Christ in the USA, and used by permission.
All rights reserved. All other Scripture quotations taken from
the Holy Bible, New International Version, copyright © 1973,
1978, 1984 International Bible Society. Used by permission of
Zondervan and Hodder & Stoughton Limited. All rights reserved.
The 'NIV' and 'New International Version' trademarks are
registered in the United States Patent and Trademark Office by
International Bible Society. Use of either trademark requires the
permission of International Bible Society. UK trademark number
1448790.

A catalogue record for this book is available
from the British Library

Typeset in 12/13 Venetian 301
Printed and bound in Singapore
05  06  07  08  09  10  10  9  8  7  6  5  4  3  2  1

# Contents

# Introduction

What is wisdom? Wisdom is probably best described as the ability to make the right choices in life. Surrounded as we are by a multiplicity of ideas and information, wisdom is as vital today as it was in ancient times.

Wisdom – *sophia* – is described in the most glowing terms in the Bible. It is more precious than rubies and confers dignity, honour, insight and prudence. Wisdom was present at the creation of the world, and Solomon, the greatest of kings, was commended for choosing wisdom over any other gift God could give. Biblical wisdom is also inextricably linked with being in relationship with God, from whom, amazingly, we can ask for this great gift. As it says in the book of James:

'If any of you lacks wisdom, he should ask God, who gives generously to all without finding fault, and it will be given to him.'

The Bible is packed with wise advice for every situation we face. I hope that you will find in the following selection some assurance that, whatever your need or experience, God is with you and will give you wisdom to know the right path for you.

Helen Jaeger

# When You Need
# *Guidance*

For attaining wisdom and discipline;
for understanding words of insight;
for acquiring a disciplined and prudent life,
doing what is right and just and fair;
for giving prudence to the simple,
knowledge and discretion to the young –
let the wise listen and add to their learning,
and let the discerning get guidance –
for understanding proverbs and parables,
the sayings and riddles of the wise.

The fear of the Lord
is the beginning of knowledge.

Proverbs 1:2–7

My son, if you accept my words
and store up my commands within you,
turning your ear to wisdom
and applying your heart to understanding,
and if you call out for insight
and cry aloud for understanding,
and if you look for it as for silver
and search for it as for hidden treasure,
then you will understand the fear of the Lord
and find the knowledge of God.
For the Lord gives wisdom,
and from his mouth come knowledge
and understanding.
He holds victory in store for the upright,
he is a shield to those whose walk is blameless,
for he guards the course of the just
and protects the way of his faithful ones.

Then you will understand what is right
and just and fair – every good path.
For wisdom will enter your heart,
and knowledge will be pleasant to your soul.

Proverbs 2:1–10


Of making many books there is no end,
and much study wearies the body.

Now all has been heard;
here is the conclusion of the matter:
Fear God and keep his commandments,
for this is the whole duty of man.

Ecclesiastes 12:12–13

But before all this,
they will lay hands on you
and persecute you.
They will deliver you
to synagogues and prisons,
and you will be brought
before kings and governors,
and all on account of my name.
This will result in your being
witnesses to them.
But make up your mind
not to worry beforehand
how you will defend yourselves.
For I will give you words and wisdom
that none of your adversaries
will be able to resist or contradict.

Luke 21:12–15


The Queen of the South will rise
at the judgment with this generation
and condemn it;
for she came from the ends of the earth
to listen to Solomon's wisdom,
and now one greater than Solomon is here.

Matthew 12:42

Then Job answered the Lord, and said,
'I know that thou canst do everything,
and that no thought can be withholden from thee.
Who is he that hideth counsel without knowledge?
therefore have I uttered that I understood not;
things too wonderful for me, which I knew not.
Hear, I beseech thee, and I will speak:
I will demand of thee, and declare thou unto me.
I have heard of thee by the hearing of the ear:
but now mine eye seeth thee.'

Job 42:1–5

Better a poor man whose walk is blameless
than a fool whose lips are perverse.

It is not good to have zeal without knowledge,
nor to be hasty and miss the way.

A man's own folly ruins his life,
yet his heart rages against the Lord.

Proverbs 19:1–3

# When You Are
# *Discouraged*

Listen, my son, accept what I say,
and the years of your life will be many.
I guide you in the way of wisdom
and lead you along straight paths.
When you walk,
your steps will not be hampered;
when you run,
you will not stumble.
Hold on to instruction,
do not let it go;
guard it well, for it is your life.

Proverbs 4:10–13

Come to me,
all of you who are tired
from carrying heavy loads,
and I will give you rest.
Take my yoke and put it on you,
and learn from me,
because I am gentle and humble in spirit;
and you will find rest.
For the yoke I will give you is easy,
and the load I will put on you is light.

Matthew 11:28–30

As you do not know the path of the wind,
or how the body is formed in a mother's womb,
so you cannot understand the work of God,
the Maker of all things.

Sow your seed in the morning,
and at evening let not your hands be idle,
for you do not know which will succeed,
whether this or that,
or whether both will do equally well.

Ecclesiastes 11:5–6

And he said,
'The kingdom of God
is as if a man should scatter seed
upon the ground,
and should sleep and rise night and day,
and the seed should sprout and grow,
he knows not how.
The earth produces of itself,
first the blade, then the ear,
then the full grain in the ear.
But when the grain is ripe,
at once he puts in the sickle,
because the harvest has come.'

And he said,
'With what can we compare
the kingdom of God,
or what parable shall we use for it?
It is like a grain of mustard seed,
which, when sown upon the ground,
is the smallest of all the seeds on earth;
yet when it is sown it grows up
and becomes the greatest of all shrubs,
and puts forth large branches,
so that the birds of the air
can make nests in its shade.'

Mark 4:26–32

He who receives you receives me,
and he who receives me
receives the one who sent me.
Anyone who receives a prophet
because he is a prophet
will receive a prophet's reward,
and anyone who receives a righteous man
because he is a righteous man
will receive a righteous man's reward.
And if anyone gives
even a cup of cold water
to one of these little ones
because he is my disciple,
I tell you the truth,
he will certainly not lose his reward.

Matthew 10:40–42

# When You Are
## *Thankful*

Behold that which I have seen:
it is good and comely
for one to eat and to drink,
and to enjoy the good of all his labour
that he taketh under the sun
all the days of his life,
which God giveth him:
for it is his portion.
Every man also
to whom God hath given riches and wealth,
and hath given him power to eat thereof,
and to take his portion,
and to rejoice in his labour;
this is the gift of God.
For he shall not
much remember the days of his life;
because God answereth him
in the joy of his heart.

Ecclesiastes 5:18–20


Sovereign Lord,
as you have promised,
you now dismiss your servant in peace.
For my eyes have seen your salvation,
which you have prepared in the sight of all people,
a light for revelation to the Gentiles
and for glory to your people Israel.

Luke 2:29–32

Shout for joy to the Lord,
all the earth.
Worship the Lord with gladness;
come before him with joyful songs.
Know that the Lord is God.
It is he who made us,
and we are his;
we are his people,
the sheep of his pasture.

Enter his gates with thanksgiving
and his courts with praise;
give thanks to him
and praise his name.

For the Lord is good
and his love endures for ever;
his faithfulness continues
through all generations.

Psalm 100


The Lord is King for ever and ever;
the nations will perish from his land.
You hear, O Lord, the desire of the afflicted;
you encourage them, and you listen to their cry,
defending the fatherless and the oppressed,
in order that man, who is of the earth,
may terrify no more.

Psalm 10:16–18

Blessed is the nation whose God is the Lord,
the people he chose for his inheritance.
From heaven the Lord looks down
and sees all mankind;
from his dwelling place he watches
all who live on earth –
he who forms the hearts of all,
who considers everything they do.
No king is saved by the size of his army;
no warrior escapes by his great strength.
A horse is a vain hope for deliverance;
despite all its great strength it cannot save.
But the eyes of the Lord are on those who fear him,
on those whose hope is in his unfailing love,
to deliver them from death
and keep them alive in famine.

We wait in hope for the Lord;
he is our help and our shield.
In him our hearts rejoice,
for we trust in his holy name.
May your unfailing love rest upon us, O Lord,
even as we put our hope in you.

Psalm 33:12–22


Praise the Lord.

Praise God in his sanctuary;
praise him in his mighty heavens.
Praise him for his acts of power;
praise him for his surpassing greatness.

Praise him with the sounding of the trumpet,
praise him with the harp and lyre,
praise him with tambourine and dancing,
praise him with the strings and flute,
praise him with the clash of cymbals,
praise him with resounding cymbals.

Let everything that has breath praise the Lord.

Praise the Lord.

Psalm 150

At that time Jesus was filled with joy
by the Holy Spirit and said,
'Father, Lord of heaven and earth!
I thank you
because you have shown
to the unlearned
what you have hidden
from the wise and learned.
Yes, Father,
this was how you wanted it to happen.
My Father has given me all things.
No one knows who the Son is
except the Father,
and no one knows who the Father is
except the Son
and those to whom the Son
chooses to reveal him.'

Then Jesus turned to the disciples
and said to them privately,
'How fortunate you are
to see the things you see!
I tell you that many prophets and kings
wanted to see what you see,
but they could not,
and to hear what you hear,
but they did not.'

Luke 10:21–24

Blessed be the Lord God of Israel,
for he has visited and redeemed his people,
and has raised up a horn of salvation for us
in the house of his servant David,
as he spoke by the mouth
of his holy prophets from of old,
that we should be saved from our enemies,
and from the hand of all who hate us;
to perform the mercy promised to our fathers,
and to remember his holy covenant,
the oath which he swore to our father Abraham,
to grant us that we,
being delivered from the hand of our enemies,
might serve him without fear,
in holiness and righteousness before him
all the days of our life.

Luke 1:68–75


Place me like a seal over your heart,
like a seal on your arm;
for love is as strong as death,
its jealousy unyielding as the grave.
It burns like blazing fire,
like a mighty flame.
Many waters cannot quench love;
rivers cannot wash it away.
If one were to give
all the wealth of his house for love,
it would be utterly scorned.

Song of Songs 8:6–7

When Elizabeth heard Mary's greeting,
the baby leaped in her womb,
and Elizabeth was filled with the Holy Spirit.
In a loud voice she exclaimed:

'Blessed are you among women,
and blessed is the child you will bear!
But why am I so favoured,
that the mother of my Lord
should come to me?
As soon as the sound of your greeting
reached my ears,
the baby in my womb leaped for joy.
Blessed is she who has believed
that what the Lord has said to her
will be accomplished!'

And Mary said:

'My soul glorifies the Lord
and my spirit rejoices in God my Saviour,
for he has been mindful of
the humble state of his servant.

From now on all generations
will call me blessed,
for the Mighty One has done great things for me –
holy is his name.
His mercy extends to those who fear him,
from generation to generation.
He has performed mighty deeds with his arm;
he has scattered those who are proud
in their inmost thoughts.

He has brought down rulers from their thrones
but has lifted up the humble.

He has filled the hungry with good things
but has sent the rich away empty.
He has helped his servant Israel,
remembering to be merciful
to Abraham and his descendants for ever,
even as he said to our fathers.'

Luke 1:41–55

# When You Are
## *Alone*

The Lord is my shepherd,
I shall not be in want.
He makes me lie down
in green pastures,
he leads me
beside quiet waters,
he restores my soul.
He guides me
in paths of righteousness
for his name's sake.
Even though I walk
through the valley
of the shadow of death,
I will fear no evil,
for you are with me;
your rod and your staff,
they comfort me.

You prepare a table before me
in the presence of my enemies.
You anoint my head with oil;
my cup overflows.
Surely goodness and love
will follow me
all the days of my life,
and I will dwell
in the house of the Lord
for ever.

Psalm 23

I am the good shepherd;
I know my sheep
and my sheep know me –
just as the Father knows me
and I know the Father –
and I lay down my life for the sheep.
I have other sheep
that are not of this sheep pen.
I must bring them also.
They too will listen to my voice,
and there shall be one flock
and one shepherd.
The reason my Father loves me
is that I lay down my life –
only to take it up again.
No one takes it from me,
but I lay it down of my own accord.
I have authority to lay it down
and authority to take it up again.
This command I received from my Father.

My sheep listen to my voice;
I know them, and they follow me.
I give them eternal life,
and they shall never perish;
no one can snatch them out of my hand.
My Father, who has given them to me,
is greater than all;
no one can snatch them out of my Father's hand.
I and the Father are one.

John 10:14–18, 27–30

If it had not been the Lord
who was on our side,
now may Israel say;
if it had not been the Lord
who was on our side,
when men rose up against us:
then they had swallowed us up quick,
when their wrath was kindled against us:
then the waters had overwhelmed us,
the stream had gone over our soul:
then the proud waters had gone over our soul.

Blessed be the Lord,
who hath not given us
as a prey to their teeth.
Our soul is escaped as a bird
out of the snare of the fowlers:
the snare is broken,
and we are escaped.

Our help is in the name of the Lord,
who made heaven and earth.

Psalm 124


'For I know the plans I have for you,'
declares the Lord,
'plans to prosper you and not to harm you,
plans to give you hope and a future.'

Jeremiah 29:11

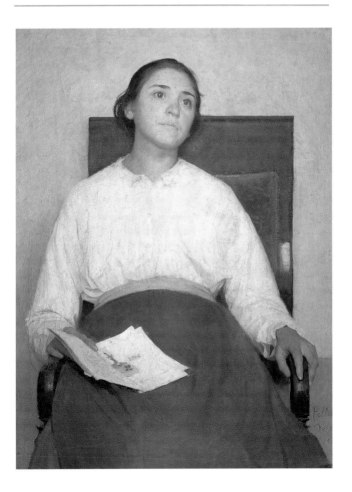

A man of many companions may come to ruin,
but there is a friend who sticks closer than a brother.

Proverbs 18:24

Listen! My lover!
Look! Here he comes,
leaping across the mountains,
bounding over the hills.
My lover is like a gazelle or a young stag.
Look! There he stands behind our wall,
gazing through the windows,
peering through the lattice.
My lover spoke and said to me,
'Arise, my darling,
my beautiful one, and come with me.
See! The winter is past;
the rains are over and gone.
Flowers appear on the earth;
the season of singing has come,
the cooing of doves
is heard in our land.
The fig tree forms its early fruit;
the blossoming vines spread their fragrance.
Arise, come, my darling;
my beautiful one, come with me.'

Song of Songs 2:8–13

All night long on my bed
I looked for the one my heart loves;
I looked for him but did not find him.
I will get up now and go about the city,
through its streets and squares;
I will search for the one my heart loves.
So I looked for him but did not find him.

The watchmen found me
as they made their rounds in the city.
'Have you seen the one my heart loves?'
Scarcely had I passed them
when I found the one my heart loves.
I held him and would not let him go
till I had brought him to my mother's house,
to the room of the one who conceived me.

Song of Songs 3:1–4

O Lord, how many are my foes!
How many rise up against me!
Many are saying of me,
'God will not deliver him.'

But you are a shield around me, O Lord;
you bestow glory on me and lift up my head.
To the Lord I cry aloud,
and he answers me from his holy hill.

I lie down and sleep;
I wake again, because the Lord sustains me.
I will not fear the tens of thousands
drawn up against me on every side.

Psalm 3:1–6


Then Jesus' mother and brothers arrived.
They stood outside the house
and sent in a message, asking for him.
A crowd was sitting round Jesus,
and they said to him,
'Look, your mother
and your brothers and sisters are outside,
and they want you.'
Jesus answered,
'Who is my mother?
Who are my brothers?'
He looked at the people sitting round him and said,
'Look! Here are my mother and my brothers!
Whoever does what God wants him to do
is my brother, my sister, my mother.'

Mark 3:31–35

If you love me,
you will obey what I command.
And I will ask the Father,
and he will give you another Counsellor
to be with you for ever –
the Spirit of truth.
The world cannot accept him,
because it neither sees him nor knows him.
But you know him,
for he lives with you
and will be in you.
I will not leave you as orphans;
I will come to you.
Before long,
the world will not see me any more,
but you will see me.
Because I live,
you also will live.
On that day you will realize
that I am in my Father,
and you are in me,
and I am in you.
Whoever has my commands
and obeys them,
he is the one who loves me.
He who loves me
will be loved by my Father,
and I too will love him
and show myself to him.

John 14:15–21

Good will come to him
who is generous and lends freely,
who conducts his affairs with justice.
Surely he will never be shaken;
a righteous man will be remembered for ever.
He will have no fear of bad news;
his heart is steadfast, trusting in the Lord.
His heart is secure, he will have no fear;
in the end he will look in triumph on his foes.

Psalm 112:5–8

# When You Are
*Waiting*

Now when Job's three friends
heard of all these troubles
that had come upon him,
each of them set out from his home –
Eliphaz the Temanite,
Bildad the Shuhite,
and Zophar the Naamathite.
They met together
to go and console and comfort him.
When they saw him from a distance,
they did not recognize him,
and they raised their voices
and wept aloud;
they tore their robes
and threw dust in the air upon their heads.
They sat with him on the ground
for seven days and seven nights,
and no one spoke a word to him,
for they saw that his suffering was very great.

Job 2:11–13


An inheritance may be gotten hastily
at the beginning;
but the end thereof shall not be blessed.

Say not thou, I will recompense evil;
but wait on the Lord, and he shall save thee.

Proverbs 20:21–22

How much longer
will you forget me, Lord?
For ever?
How much longer
will you hide yourself from me?
How long must I endure trouble?
How long will sorrow
fill my heart day and night?
How long will my enemies
triumph over me?

Look at me, O Lord my God,
and answer me.
Restore my strength;
don't let me die.
Don't let my enemies say,
'We have defeated him.'
Don't let them gloat over my downfall.

I rely on your constant love;
I will be glad,
because you will rescue me.
I will sing to you, O Lord,
because you have been good to me.

Psalm 13

Like cold water to a weary soul
is good news from a distant land.

Proverbs 25:25

I waited patiently for the Lord;
he turned to me and heard my cry.
He lifted me out of the slimy pit,
out of the mud and mire;
he set my feet on a rock
and gave me a firm place to stand.

He put a new song in my mouth,
a hymn of praise to our God.
Many will see and fear
and put their trust in the Lord.

Blessed is the man
who makes the Lord his trust,
who does not look to the proud,
to those who turn aside to false gods.
Many, O Lord my God,
are the wonders you have done.
The things you planned for us
no one can recount to you;
were I to speak and tell of them,
they would be too many to declare.

Psalm 40:1–5

See how the farmer waits
for the land to yield its valuable crop
and how patient he is
for the autumn and spring rains.
You too, be patient and stand firm,
because the Lord's coming is near.

As you know, we consider blessed
those who have persevered.
You have heard of Job's perseverance
and have seen what the Lord
finally brought about.
The Lord is full of compassion and mercy.

James 5:7–8, 11

Then shall the kingdom of heaven
be likened unto ten virgins,
which took their lamps,
and went forth to meet the bridegroom.
And five of them were wise,
and five were foolish.
They that were foolish took their lamps,
and took no oil with them:
but the wise took oil in their vessels
with their lamps.

While the bridegroom tarried,
they all slumbered and slept.
And at midnight there was a cry made,
'Behold, the bridegroom cometh;
go ye out to meet him.'
Then all those virgins arose,
and trimmed their lamps.
And the foolish said unto the wise,
'Give us of your oil;
for our lamps are gone out.'
But the wise answered, saying,
'Not so;
lest there be not enough for us and you:
but go ye rather to them that sell,
and buy for yourselves.'
And while they went to buy,
the bridegroom came;
and they that were ready
went in with him to the marriage:
and the door was shut.

Afterward came also the other virgins,
saying, 'Lord, Lord, open to us.'
But he answered and said,
'Verily I say unto you,
I know you not.'
Watch therefore,
for ye know neither the day nor the hour
wherein the Son of man cometh.

Matthew 25:1–13

There was a man who had two sons.
The younger one said to his father,
'Father, give me my share of the estate.'
So he divided his property between them.

Not long after that,
the younger son got together all he had,
set off for a distant country
and there squandered his wealth in wild living.
After he had spent everything,
there was a severe famine in that whole country,
and he began to be in need.
So he went and hired himself out
to a citizen of that country,
who sent him to his fields to feed pigs.
He longed to fill his stomach
with the pods that the pigs were eating,
but no one gave him anything.

When he came to his senses, he said,
'How many of my father's hired men
have food to spare,
and here I am starving to death!
I will set out and go back to my father
and say to him:
Father, I have sinned against heaven
and against you.
I am no longer worthy to be called your son;
make me like one of your hired men.'
So he got up and went to his father.

But while he was still a long way off,
his father saw him
and was filled with compassion for him;
he ran to his son,
threw his arms around him and kissed him.

The son said to him,
'Father, I have sinned against heaven
and against you.
I am no longer worthy to be called your son.'

But the father said to his servants,
'Quick! Bring the best robe and put it on him.
Put a ring on his finger and sandals on his feet.
Bring the fattened calf and kill it.
Let's have a feast and celebrate.
For this son of mine was dead and is alive again;
he was lost and is found.'
So they began to celebrate.

Luke 15:11–24

# When You Are

# *Afraid*

The Lord is my light and my salvation;
whom shall I fear?
the Lord is the strength of my life;
of whom shall I be afraid?
When the wicked,
even mine enemies and my foes,
came upon me to eat up my flesh,
they stumbled and fell.
Though an host should encamp against me,
my heart shall not fear:
though war should rise against me,
in this will I be confident.
One thing have I desired of the Lord,
that will I seek after;
that I may dwell in the house of the Lord
all the days of my life,
to behold the beauty of the Lord,
and to inquire in his temple.
For in the time of trouble
he shall hide me in his pavilion:
in the secret of his tabernacle
shall he hide me;
he shall set me up upon a rock.

Psalm 27:1–5

My son,
preserve sound judgment and discernment,
do not let them out of your sight;
they will be life for you,
an ornament to grace your neck.
Then you will go on your way in safety,
and your foot will not stumble;
when you lie down, you will not be afraid;
when you lie down, your sleep will be sweet.
Have no fear of sudden disaster
or of the ruin that overtakes the wicked,
for the Lord will be your confidence
and will keep your foot from being snared.

Proverbs 3:21–26


When the sentence for a crime
is not quickly carried out,
the hearts of the people
are filled with schemes to do wrong.
Although a wicked man
commits a hundred crimes
and still lives a long time,
I know that it will go better
with God-fearing men,
who are reverent before God.
Yet because the wicked do not fear God,
it will not go well with them,
and their days will not lengthen like a shadow.

Ecclesiastes 8:11–13

On that day, when evening had come,
he said to them,
'Let us go across to the other side.'
And leaving the crowd,
they took him with them in the boat,
just as he was.
And other boats were with him.
And a great storm of wind arose,
and the waves beat into the boat,
so that the boat was already filling.
But he was in the stern,
asleep on the cushion;
and they woke him and said to him,
'Teacher, do you not care if we perish?'

And he awoke and rebuked the wind,
and said to the sea,
'Peace! Be still!'
And the wind ceased,
and there was a great calm.
He said to them,
'Why are you afraid?
Have you no faith?'
And they were filled with awe,
and said to one another,
'Who then is this,
that even wind and sea obey him?'

Mark 4:35–41

Do not be afraid of those
who kill the body
but cannot kill the soul.
Rather, be afraid of the One
who can destroy both soul and body in hell.
Are not two sparrows sold for a penny?
Yet not one of them will fall to the ground
apart from the will of your Father.
And even the very hairs of your head
are all numbered.
So don't be afraid;
you are worth more than many sparrows.

Matthew 10:28–31

So I say to you,
Ask, and it will be given to you;
search, and you will find;
knock, and the door will be opened for you.
For everyone who asks receives,
and everyone who searches finds,
and for everyone who knocks,
the door will be opened.
Is there anyone among you who,
if your child asks for a fish,
will give a snake instead of a fish?
Or if the child asks for an egg,
will give a scorpion?
If you then, who are evil,
know how to give good gifts to your children,
how much more will the heavenly Father
give the Holy Spirit to those who ask him!

Luke 11:9–13

Peter answered him,
'We have left everything to follow you!
What then will there be for us?'
Jesus said to them,
'I tell you the truth,
at the renewal of all things,
when the Son of Man
sits on his glorious throne,
you who have followed me
will also sit on twelve thrones,
judging the twelve tribes of Israel.

And everyone who has left houses
or brothers or sisters or father or mother
or children or fields for my sake
will receive a hundred times as much
and will inherit eternal life.'

Matthew 19:27–29

This is why I tell you not to be worried
about the food and drink you need
in order to stay alive,
or about clothes for your body.
After all, isn't life worth more than food?
And isn't the body worth more than clothes?
Look at the birds:
they do not sow seeds,
gather a harvest and put it in barns;
yet your Father in heaven takes care of them!
Aren't you worth much more than birds?
Can any of you live a bit longer
by worrying about it?
And why worry about clothes?
Look how the wild flowers grow:
they do not work
or make clothes for themselves.
But I tell you that not even King Solomon
with all his wealth had clothes
as beautiful as one of these flowers.
It is God who clothes the wild grass –
grass that is here today and gone tomorrow,
burned up in the oven.
Won't he be all the more sure to clothe you?
How little faith you have!
So do not start worrying:
'Where will my food come from?
or my drink? or my clothes?'
Your Father in heaven knows
that you need all these things.

Instead, be concerned above everything else
with the Kingdom of God
and with what he requires of you,
and he will provide you
with all these other things.
So do not worry about tomorrow;
it will have enough worries of its own.
There is no need to add to the troubles
each day brings.

Matthew 6:25–34

# When You Are
# *Facing Change*

To everything there is a season,
and a time to every purpose under the heaven:
a time to be born,
and a time to die;
a time to plant,
and a time to pluck up that which is planted;
a time to kill,
and a time to heal;
a time to break down,
and a time to build up;
a time to weep,
and a time to laugh;

a time to mourn,
and a time to dance;
a time to cast away stones,
and a time to gather stones together;
a time to embrace,
and a time to refrain from embracing;
a time to get,
and a time to lose;
a time to keep,
and a time to cast away;
a time to rend,
and a time to sew;
a time to keep silence,
and a time to speak;
a time to love,
and a time to hate;
a time of war,
and a time of peace.

Ecclesiastes 3:1–8

Consider what God has done:

Who can straighten
what he has made crooked?
When times are good, be happy;
but when times are bad, consider:
God has made the one
as well as the other.

Ecclesiastes 7:13–14

Whatever exists
has already been named,
and what man is
has been known;
no man can contend
with one who is stronger than he.
The more the words,
the less the meaning,
and how does that profit anyone?

For who knows
what is good for a man in life,
during the few and meaningless days
he passes through like a shadow?
Who can tell him
what will happen under the sun
after he is gone?

Ecclesiastes 6:10–12

He then began to teach them
that the Son of Man
must suffer many things
and be rejected by the elders,
chief priests and teachers of the law,
and that he must be killed
and after three days rise again.
He spoke plainly about this,
and Peter took him aside
and began to rebuke him.

But when Jesus turned
and looked at his disciples,
he rebuked Peter.
'Get behind me, Satan!' he said.
'You do not have in mind
the things of God,
but the things of men.'

Mark 8:31–33


And Jesus began to say to them,
'Take heed that no one leads you astray.
Many will come in my name, saying,
'I am he!'
and they will lead many astray.
And when you hear of wars
and rumours of wars,
do not be alarmed;
this must take place,
but the end is not yet.
For nation will rise against nation,
and kingdom against kingdom;
there will be earthquakes in various places,
there will be famines;
this is but the beginning
of the birth pangs.

Mark 13:5–8

Trust in the Lord
with all your heart.
Never rely on
what you think you know.
Remember the Lord
in everything you do,
and he will show you the right way.
Never let yourself think
that you are wiser than you are;
simply obey the Lord
and refuse to do wrong.
If you do,
it will be like good medicine,
healing your wounds
and easing your pains.

Proverbs 3:5–8


Let not your heart be troubled:
ye believe in God,
believe also in me.
In my Father's house
are many mansions:
if it were not so, I would have told you.
I go to prepare a place for you.
And if I go and prepare a place for you,
I will come again,
and receive you unto myself;
that where I am, there ye may be also.

John 14:1–3

Peace I leave with you;
my peace I give you.
I do not give to you as the world gives.
Do not let your hearts be troubled
and do not be afraid.
You heard me say,
'I am going away
and I am coming back to you.'
If you loved me,
you would be glad
that I am going to the Father,
for the Father is greater than I.

John 14:27–28

Better a patient man
than a warrior,
a man who controls his temper
than one who takes a city.

The lot is cast into the lap,
but its every decision is from the Lord.

Proverbs 16:32–33

# When You Are

# *Suffering*

And I saw something else under the sun:

In the place of judgment —
wickedness was there,
in the place of justice —
wickedness was there.

I thought in my heart,

'God will bring to judgment
both the righteous and the wicked,
for there will be a time for every activity,
a time for every deed.'

I also thought,

'As for men,
God tests them
so that they may see
that they are like the animals.
Man's fate is like that
of the animals;
the same fate awaits them both:
as one dies, so dies the other.
All have the same breath;
man has no advantage
over the animal.
Everything is meaningless.
All go to the same place;
all come from dust,
and to dust all return.
Who knows if the spirit of man
rises upward
and if the spirit of the animal
goes down into the earth?'

So I saw
that there is nothing better for a man
than to enjoy his work,
because that is his lot.
For who can bring him to see
what will happen after him?

Ecclesiastes 3:16–22

Now when he saw the crowds,
he went up on a mountainside and sat down.
His disciples came to him,
and he began to teach them, saying:

'Blessed are the poor in spirit,
for theirs is the kingdom of heaven.
Blessed are those who mourn,
for they will be comforted.
Blessed are the meek,
for they will inherit the earth.
Blessed are those
who hunger and thirst for righteousness,
for they will be filled.
Blessed are the merciful,
for they will be shown mercy.
Blessed are the pure in heart,
for they will see God.
Blessed are the peacemakers,
for they will be called sons of God.
Blessed are those who are persecuted
because of righteousness,
for theirs is the kingdom of heaven.

Blessed are you when people insult you,
persecute you and falsely say
all kinds of evil against you because of me.
Rejoice and be glad,
because great is your reward in heaven,
for in the same way
they persecuted the prophets
who were before you.'

Matthew 5:1–12

I remember my affliction and my wandering,
the bitterness and the gall.
I will remember them,
and my soul is downcast within me.
Yet this I call to mind
and therefore I have hope:

Because of the Lord's great love
we are not consumed,
for his compassions never fail.
They are new every morning;
great is your faithfulness.

Lamentations 3:19–23

Blessed is he
who considers the poor!
The Lord delivers him
in the day of trouble;
the Lord protects him
and keeps him alive;
he is called blessed in the land;
thou dost not give him up
to the will of his enemies.
The Lord sustains him
on his sickbed;
in his illness thou healest
all his infirmities.

Psalm 41:1–3

A large crowd followed
and pressed around him.
And a woman was there
who had been subject to bleeding
for twelve years.
She had suffered a great deal
under the care of many doctors
and had spent all she had,
yet instead of getting better
she grew worse.
When she heard about Jesus,
she came up behind him in the crowd
and touched his cloak,

because she thought,
'If I just touch his clothes,
I will be healed.'
Immediately her bleeding stopped
and she felt in her body
that she was freed from her suffering.

At once Jesus realized
that power had gone out from him.
He turned around in the crowd and asked,
'Who touched my clothes?'

'You see the people
crowding against you,'
his disciples answered,
'and yet you can ask,
"Who touched me?" '

But Jesus kept looking around
to see who had done it.
Then the woman,
knowing what had happened to her,
came and fell at his feet
and, trembling with fear,
told him the whole truth.
He said to her,
'Daughter, your faith has healed you.
Go in peace
and be freed from your suffering.'

Mark 5:24–34

As he went along,
he saw a man blind from birth.
His disciples asked him,
'Rabbi, who sinned,
this man or his parents,
that he was born blind?'
'Neither this man
nor his parents sinned,'
said Jesus, 'but this happened
so that the work of God
might be displayed in his life.'

John 9:1–3

At this, Job got up
and tore his robe and shaved his head.
Then he fell to the ground
in worship and said:

'Naked I came from my mother's womb,
and naked I shall depart.
The Lord gave
and the Lord has taken away;
may the name of the Lord be praised.'

In all this, Job did not sin
by charging God with wrongdoing.

Job 1:20–22

Better to be lowly in spirit
and among the oppressed
than to share plunder with the proud.

Proverbs 16:19

When I said,
'My foot is slipping,'
your love, O Lord, supported me.
When anxiety was great within me,
your consolation brought joy
to my soul.

Psalm 94:18–19

When the Lord corrects you, my son,
pay close attention
and take it as a warning.
The Lord corrects those he loves,
as parents correct a child
of whom they are proud.

Proverbs 3:11–12

# When You Are
## *At Rest*

My soul finds rest in God alone;
my salvation comes from him.
He alone is my rock and my salvation;
he is my fortress, I shall never be shaken.

How long will you assault a man?
Would all of you throw him down –
this leaning wall, this tottering fence?
They fully intend to topple him
from his lofty place;
they take delight in lies.
With their mouths they bless,
but in their hearts they curse.

Find rest, O my soul, in God alone;
my hope comes from him.
He alone is my rock and my salvation;
he is my fortress, I shall not be shaken.
My salvation and my honour depend on God;
he is my mighty rock, my refuge.
Trust in him at all times, O people;
pour out your hearts to him,
for God is our refuge.

Psalm 62:1–8


Be wise enough
not to wear yourself out trying to get rich.
Your money can be gone in a flash,
as if it had grown wings
and flown away like an eagle.

Proverbs 23:4–5

When goods increase,
they increase who eat them;
and what gain has their owner
but to see them with his eyes?
Sweet is the sleep of a labourer,
whether he eats little or much;
but the surfeit of the rich
will not let him sleep.

Ecclesiastes 5:11–12

Whoever goes to the Lord for safety,
whoever remains under the protection
of the Almighty, can say to him,
'You are my defender and protector.
You are my God; in you I trust.'
He will keep you safe
from all hidden dangers
and from all deadly diseases.
He will cover you with his wings;
you will be safe in his care;
his faithfulness will protect and defend you.
You need not fear any dangers at night
or sudden attacks during the day
or the plagues that strike in the dark
or the evils that kill in daylight.

A thousand may fall dead beside you,
ten thousand all round you,
but you will not be harmed.
You will look and see
how the wicked are punished.

Psalm 91:1–8

The fear of the Lord
leads to life:
then one rests content,
untouched by trouble.

Proverbs 19:23

O Jerusalem, Jerusalem,
you who kill the prophets
and stone those sent to you,
how often I have longed
to gather your children together,
as a hen gathers her chicks under her wings,
but you were not willing.

Matthew 23:37

He that hath knowledge spareth his words:
and a man of understanding
is of an excellent spirit.
Even a fool, when he holdeth his peace,
is counted wise:
and he that shutteth his lips
is esteemed a man of understanding.

Proverbs 17:27–28


You have made the Lord your defender,
the Most High your protector,
and so no disaster will strike you,
no violence will come near your home.
God will put his angels in charge of you
to protect you wherever you go.
They will hold you up with their hands
to keep you from hurting your feet on the stones.
You will trample down lions and snakes,
fierce lions and poisonous snakes.

God says, 'I will save those who love me
and will protect those who acknowledge me as Lord.
When they call to me, I will answer them;
when they are in trouble, I will be with them.
I will rescue them and honour them.
I will reward them with long life;
I will save them.'

Psalm 91:9–16

I am the true vine,
and my Father is the vine-grower.
He removes every branch in me
that bears no fruit.
Every branch that bears fruit he prunes
to make it bear more fruit.
You have already been cleansed
by the word that I have spoken to you.
Abide in me as I abide in you.
Just as the branch cannot bear fruit by itself
unless it abides in the vine,
neither can you unless you abide in me.
I am the vine, you are the branches.
Those who abide in me and I in them
bear much fruit,
because apart from me you can do nothing.
Whoever does not abide in me
is thrown away like a branch and withers;
such branches are gathered,
thrown into the fire, and burned.
If you abide in me, and my words abide in you,
ask for whatever you wish,
and it will be done for you.
My Father is glorified by this,
that you bear much fruit
and become my disciples.

John 15:1–8

Wisdom, like an inheritance,
is a good thing
and benefits those who see the sun.
Wisdom is a shelter
as money is a shelter,
but the advantage of knowledge is this:
that wisdom preserves the life
of its possessor.

Ecclesiastes 7:11–12

# When You Are

## *Joyful*

Which one of you, having a hundred sheep
and losing one of them,
does not leave the ninety-nine
in the wilderness
and go after the one that is lost
until he finds it?
When he has found it,
he lays it on his shoulders and rejoices.
And when he comes home,
he calls together his friends and neighbours,
saying to them,
'Rejoice with me,
for I have found my sheep that was lost.'

Luke 15:4–6

Or suppose a woman has ten silver coins
and loses one.
Does she not light a lamp,
sweep the house and search carefully
until she finds it?
And when she finds it,
she calls her friends and neighbours together
and says,
'Rejoice with me;
I have found my lost coin.'
In the same way, I tell you,
there is rejoicing
in the presence of the angels of God
over one sinner who repents.

Luke 15:8–10

In his heart a man plans his course,
but the Lord determines his steps.

Proverbs 16:9

Light is sweet,
and it pleases the eyes to see the sun.
However many years a man may live,
let him enjoy them all.
But let him remember the days of darkness,
for they will be many.

Be happy, young man,
while you are young,
and let your heart give you joy
in the days of your youth.
Follow the ways of your heart
and whatever your eyes see,
but know that for all these things
God will bring you to judgment.
So then, banish anxiety from your heart
and cast off the troubles of your body.

Ecclesiastes 11:7–10


When the Lord brought back
the captives to Zion,
we were like men who dreamed.
Our mouths were filled with laughter,
our tongues with songs of joy.
Then it was said among the nations,
'The Lord has done great things for them.'
The Lord has done great things for us,
and we are filled with joy.

Restore our fortunes, O Lord,
like streams in the Negev.
Those who sow in tears
will reap with songs of joy.
He who goes out weeping,
carrying seed to sow,
will return with songs of joy,
carrying sheaves with him.

Psalm 126

I know that there is nothing better for men
than to be happy and do good while they live.
That everyone may eat and drink,
and find satisfaction in all his toil –
this is the gift of God.
I know that everything God does
will endure for ever;
nothing can be added to it
and nothing taken from it.
God does it so that men will revere him.

Ecclesiastes 3:12–14


When I was a boy in my father's house,
still tender, and an only child of my mother,
he taught me and said,
'Lay hold of my words with all your heart;
keep my commands and you will live.
Get wisdom, get understanding;
do not forget my words or swerve from them.
Do not forsake wisdom, and she will protect you;
love her, and she will watch over you.
Wisdom is supreme; therefore get wisdom.
Though it cost all you have, get understanding.
Esteem her, and she will exalt you;
embrace her, and she will honour you.
She will set a garland of grace on your head
and present you with a crown of splendour.'

Proverbs 4:3–9

Thus says the Lord:
In a time of favour I have answered you,
on a day of salvation I have helped you;
I have kept you and given you
as a covenant to the people,
to establish the land,
to apportion the desolate heritages;
saying to the prisoners,
'Come out,'
to those who are in darkness,
'Show yourselves.'
They shall feed along the ways,
on all the bare heights shall be their pasture;
they shall not hunger or thirst,
neither scorching wind nor sun
shall strike them down,
for he who has pity on them will lead them,
and by springs of water will guide them.
And I will turn all my mountains into a road,
and my highways shall be raised up.
Lo, these shall come from far away,
and lo, these from the north and from the west,
and these from the land of Syene.

Sing for joy, O heavens, and exult, O earth;
break forth, O mountains, into singing!
For the Lord has comforted his people,
and will have compassion on his suffering ones.

Isaiah 49:8–13

And there were in the same country
shepherds abiding in the field,
keeping watch over their flock by night.

And, lo,
the angel of the Lord came upon them,
and the glory of the Lord
shone round about them:
and they were sore afraid.

And the angel said unto them,
'Fear not: for, behold,
I bring you good tidings of great joy,
which shall be to all people.
For unto you is born this day
in the city of David a Saviour,
which is Christ the Lord.
And this shall be a sign unto you;
Ye shall find the babe
wrapped in swaddling clothes,
lying in a manger.'

And suddenly there was with the angel
a multitude of the heavenly host praising God,
and saying,
'Glory to God in the highest,
and on earth peace,
good will toward men.'

Luke 2:8–14

Suddenly the Lord himself
stood among them and said to them,
'Peace be with you.'
They were terrified,
thinking that they were seeing a ghost.
But he said to them,
'Why are you alarmed?
Why are these doubts coming up in your minds?
Look at my hands and my feet,
and see that it is I myself.
Feel me, and you will know,
for a ghost doesn't have flesh and bones,
as you can see I have.'
He said this
and showed them his hands and his feet.
They still could not believe,
they were so full of joy and wonder;
so he asked them,
'Have you anything here to eat?'
They gave him a piece of cooked fish,
which he took and ate in their presence.

Then he led them out of the city as far as Bethany,
where he raised his hands and blessed them.
As he was blessing them,
he departed from them
and was taken up into heaven.
They worshipped him and went back into Jerusalem,
filled with great joy,
and spent all their time in the Temple
giving thanks to God.

Luke 24:36–43, 50–53